A
Life's
Heart

By
Steven Thomas

Table of Contents:

A Way Out

Why do we look for an escape?

To find a way out of this place.

When it all seems to fade away,

We give up on everything that comes our way.

When no one understands what's inside,

You feel like you're trapped in life.

The world around you slowly caves in,

You just want to start over, begin.

When you think it's all gone with nothing left,

You want to look up and take your last breath.

You think it'd be better if you weren't
here,

It would shatter lives if you
disappeared.

Drifting off into the other world,
which we cannot see,

To know that's a safer place,
somewhere where I believe.

To look for the answers when life gets
hard,

They can be found without being
scarred.

Take the time out of your day,

To get on your knees and simply pray.

<u>Alone</u>

Being in this world, lonesome as can
be,

With no one else around, just lonely
me.

Through these eyes, oh what I see,

Is a life I face that's hard to believe?

Having everything stripped from
underneath,

While I walk this ground on my own
two feet.

With every step taken, it feels like a
dream,

But I know this is life with all its
reality.

Looking on with every breath I breathe,

Watching it all slip away from beneath.

Feeling as if there's nothing left,

Only to think if I have this life to regret.

Living for what I thought I knew,

Seeing it only to be what I find true.

Life isn't easy when you're alone,

When you have no one to fall back on.

Even though I may stand by myself,

As I live with this hand that I'm dealt.

I know there's someone higher looking down,

Watching over me as I carry on with a smile, not a frown.

<u>Always There</u>

As I stare up in the sky,

I feel a gleam in my eye.

I begin to think of you,

Pretending to know what I thought I
knew.

When I see your face through my eyes,

I feel a tear form inside.

The tears of pain are not to hide,

Releasing them is a way of healing, no
deny.

When I do look up to the sky,

I see the clouds with an outline.

A figure of you appears in a certain
way,

Reminding me of your promise of faith.

When I look up to the heavens above,

All I can think about is all your love.

Seeing your face brings tears to my eyes,

When I didn't even have a chance to say "good-bye".

So I close my eyes and bow my head,

Saying a prayer of the things I should've said.

Anniversary

A...s I look into your eyes

N...othing seems to ever compare

N...othing will ever keep us apart

I...n this world of hard times and despair

V...ery much in love with you, can't get enough

E...verything may seem to drag us down

R...eaching out for a hand with that loving touch

S...taring at one another with nothing in sound

A...ppearing as if we found our soul mate

R...ight out in front us, if we only opened our eyes

y...ou are the one for me and that will never break

<u>Blind</u>

People tend to look at me,
I try to figure out who they see.
Is it someone they can judge quickly?
Or do they see me as a human being.

Seeing myself through their eyes,
Wondering if they would ever despise
Me for who I really am,
And accept me as a man.

Sometimes I can't help but feel the
pain,
It's just something hard to explain.
Is it caused by myself or by other's,
So I just live, deal, and suffer.

My heart races with fear inside,

Thinking I'm just going to be denied.

By the way I look or by the things I say,

Why do people have to be that way?

When they shake their head and turn away,

I feel there's nothing left for me to stay.

I can't change the way I was made,

So I shall live with it until my grave.

Breaking the Silence

Growing up, the things you hear,

Can't compare to the things you see.

Hearing the voices of the ones you
love,

Hurtful tears you see, leaves you
where it's hard to breath.

Listening to words that cut like a
knife,

Leaving you scarred the rest of your
life.

Seeing the emotions of one another,

Breaks you down, feeling weaker like
no other.

Where it places you is somewhere so
dark,

You want to be okay with it all, but you're torn apart.

A place that you can't begin to explain,

Something inside won't let go of the pain.

Now you've carried on through the years,

Hiding within is all the hidden tears.

You never thought you'd be where you're at,

Having the strength to hold on and not to collapse.

Broken Trust

Every now and then I think how it
used to be,

In all the ways I trusted, the ways I
believed.

Now every time I look at you,

Is something now I could never do.

Through my eyes, the things I'd see,

What could be, are things needed for
eternity.

In my mind I believed your lies,

Thinking why you spoke to me
deceptively.

To hear.....

Your promised lies, your broken
words

Things you said to me with all lost honesty.

If you only knew what you put me through,

The secret emotions you never knew.

Hiding so deep are feelings from inside,

Every time I think about it, I want to cry.

Memories alone, they fade away,

Somewhere to a darker place.

Somewhere where there is no faith,

A place that I find I can't erase.

Buried

Climbing out of the depths
underneath,

Where I can just find a place to see.

Somewhere there's a place with
means,

Other than here on the grounds
beneath.

Wanting to plant to the earth below,

The feet I have for people to know.

I dig and I claw for what I believe,

Somehow I see people don't believe in
me.

As the darkness surrounds me in my
dreams,

Living a life with no other means.

I find it all hard to overcome,

Finding myself becoming numb.

Reaching for this life to live,

What else is there to give?

Than what I already have portrayed,

Giving more than what's already been made.

Do I deserve this life I am living?

Or is there something better to have faith in?

Knowing I may never have this life to live again,

Even though I know this life I live is full of sin.

<u>Days</u>

When I wake up, you're always on my mind,

Knowing I'm on yours, makes me feel good inside.

The first thing I hear is the sweetness of your voice,

When there is nothing else more I want, even with a choice.

I start my day with a smile on my face,

Knowing there's one on yours, I would never replace.

Every day I live I love you more and more,

Every single minute, I love you more than before.

Throughout the day, I think of how you love me so,

Having that feeling within, it will always be known.

To know that you will forever be true,

Will always be with me, never to lose.

As the day comes to an end, you in my heart I will hold,

Forever to be with you is more priceless than gold.

The love you have for me, from which I see,

Is beyond this life, through eternity.

In my dreams you will forever be,

All I want to do is make you happy.

When in my dreams, I hope you look to find,

That my love for you will always
have a shine.

My heart melts with thoughts of you,

May it forever last with no chance of
being through.

I know you feel the same way as me,

Shall the love we have together
forever be.

Distant World

Underneath my feet, I walk the earth
beneath,

Walking the silent footsteps of what I
falsely believe.

My legs start to tremble as I fall down
to my knees,

With thoughts so deep, I feel as though
they could bleed.

Trying to overcome of this fear of
hope,

When there's nothing there, but
shattered faith below.

Seeing the rays of fate slowly slip
away,

Wondering if I'll survive to see
another day.

Living with broken promises and
empty dreams,

Watching life go by with this built up
misery.

Should I give up on what I have
completely?

Or fight to live for this lonely reality.

Seeing a world in shades of gray,

Through the eyes of one gone astray.

Lost within hoping to be found,

With two feet planted on solid ground.

Element of Love

To the love of my life, where have you been?

I know I'll never have to search again.

To know you're on my mind and in my heart,

Waiting for the day we'll never be apart.

Every feeling I have inside of me,

Is given to you with every word I breath.

The beating of my heart only beats for you,

Every ounce of love I have for you is true.

I never knew it was possible to love someone this much,

Making us crave one another's caring touch.

Two souls brought together to make us complete,

Just when we both decided to accept defeat.

The love we have for each other is pure and strong,

Everything we've been wanting and wishing for all along.

We can make it through anything if we just stick together,

No doubt in my mind we'll be together forever.

When the sun is out with brightest clouds of white,

And when the darkness comes and darkens them with night,

With the moonlight shining I see them being outlined,

I never will forget my love for you, it'll always be out-shined.

The space between us will soon be gone,

As our love gives us strength to carry on.

It's so strong and deep within our hearts,

Looking forward to hear you recite, "Until death do us part".

Everlasting Love

From the time I heard your voice
with the words you said,

I listened to your heart and something
inside of me bled.

I knew from the start, I didn't want to
be with anyone else,

You opened up a part of me that I
never would've seen myself.

This love you brought out of me that
now shows on the surface,

Was buried so deep within, begging to
be released for this purpose.

Digging so far down, never did I think
I'd reach so deep,

Now that I have, you've shown me
how to sincerely believe.

As you opened my eyes to something
underneath my skin,

I would never want to give it up and
start over again.

Oh, so many times I was about to
regret this life within,

After I met you, it all made sense as
to where I am to begin.

With my love for you flowing like a
river into the ocean,

Nothing can be better than the time of
our devotion.

Love I've gave to others, only trickled
like a dripping faucet,

I now know what true love is and I
will never forget it.

There is so much meaning behind the
words of ones love,

For me it stretches beyond the skies so far above.

For some it's only as far as they can see,

And for others, love can be as blind as can be.

Everything I am inside and out,

You have earned with your love, no doubt.

Giving me everything you are in return,

I still have a lot in life to learn.

So here we are together again at last,

Never again do I want to be out of your grasp.

Through this time we've had, loneliness will surpass,

Forever we will be together and always outlast life's mishaps.

<u>Eyes of Faith</u>

Often times we see things in life only
for what they can be,

Sometimes we look at it through the
eyes of negativity.

Focusing on doubts of life's little
worries,

Letting it get down inside to the core
of we.

Seeing the things only you could
dream,

Wondering if they will ever become a
reality.

You can accomplish your goals if you
only believe,

Without fear holding you back from
what you can achieve.

Listening and hearing the things people say,

Can lift you up or tear you down, either way.

Filling your mind with good or bad,

Makes you think of the life we have.

The way we live we may accept,

Maybe it's one you might reject.

It can be in a place where you're content,

Maybe your world has never had a dent.

Staying in faith is something hard to do,

When you know all that you've been through.

Feeling as if it was falling to pieces,

Our faith within slowly decreases.

Remembering this one thing, never to
forget,
This life you have is not one to regret.
We are here for a purpose untold,
Watching God guide us as we unfold.

Facing the Edge

Living a life with everything in place
and so content,

Couldn't ask for more when it seems
straight without a dent.

Until one mistake comes along and it
all becomes disturbed,

Wanting to speak out, but nothing you
say can be heard.

Carrying on through this world with
bothersome trials,

Knowing there are others living
around you with smiles.

You know what you've done and know
what has happened,

But on the inside you feel nothing but
being trapped.

*You put on a front and wear a smile
to make it not known,*

*On the other hand, it's hurting you so
bad you feel lesser grown.*

*It's eating you up on the inside and
soon becomes a reality,*

*Signs and symptoms start to show and
you think of your own mortality.*

*Keeping it a secret from loved ones so
they don't feel the pain,*

*But it gets worse and they wonder
what is going on to help you remain.*

*The feeling of hurting others is
something you never want to do,*

*Sometimes the truth has to come out
to get support to pull through.*

*Not telling your family just wanting
to take care of them first,*

Putting them before yourself before you start to get worse.

Making sure they're okay so they can take care of themselves,

Now that they can, you can focus on helping the one that matters, yourself.

God is watching over us and will bring us through all this tribulation,

Even though we all endure some sort of aggravation and frustration.

He blesses those who are in need as long as we pray and give thanks,

God knows all and fills every need we have without leaving blanks.

Falling

When you're alone and longing for
someone special,

Getting hurt over and over again
becomes old and brittle.

You look most of your life but no one
suits your needs,

You stop and close your eyes with a
need to breathe.

When you need to be in a place far
from any sound,

Clearing your mind from all the
negativity around.

You open a new door to only find to
see,

That someone in front of you, smiling
with glee.

Eyes fill with tears as you hear those
special words,

Crying out for so long, never knowing
how close you were.

Those words that can only fill a heart
with joy,

Holding on to what you give each
other, never to destroy.

Having that in your life, nothing
could ever replace,

For it is there all around you like
unending space.

There is only one way I can say what
it can be,

Love is the greatest thing you've given
someone like me.

Fear

Growing up in a home so disturbed
and discreet,

No one ever knew of the life of one
being obsolete.

Feeling like there's no one there to
confide in,

Thinking there's only one thing that
could end.

You break me down so much to where
I can't stand,

You think you can tear me down
because you're a man.

Living in this life is a constant
struggle,

If you only knew what you brought
upon me, you'd grovel

As I....

Fear the days I'm soon to see,

I know they'll be in my memories.

With nothing but regrets I hold inside,

I carry them with me through-out my life.

Growing up....

I realize that I'm someone who doesn't deserve what I'm given,

There's something better out there, something worth to believe in.

Stricken by words will I never forget,

Poisoned by what I have experienced.

With you....

Now I see what it means to be,

Happy, content and where I can see.

That I belong in this world,

With no more times in a swirl.

From now on...

I'll respect you for who God made you,

Knowing that you will always be
what you knew.

With everything brought into life's
perspective,

You wonder if I will ever forgive.

First Sight

From time to time we glanced at one another,

I saw something in you nothing like no other.

Someone with beauty inside and out,

You'll always have that without a doubt.

As I look in your eyes, I could forever stare,

That sparkle I see, I could never compare.

Seeing a look no one else could ever have,

Is something I'll cherish until the day I pass.

To see a smile on your face,

Brings happiness and joy every day,

With words alone I will always say,

Those few moments I would never
replace.

Flesh and Bone

Living with this outer exterior of
what God has made,

I shall live with it until my grave.

Until then I will live with what spirit
has been given,

Making the best of it and how I
believe.

With all the troubles in the world, He
always brings me through,

No matter how many times I fall, He
picks me up and pulls me to.

Slipping and stumbling on throughout
this life of mine,

One day I know I am to forever stand
out and shine.

Having this body that I am embedded
with,

I am to forever have with flaws only
to be forgiven.

Mistakes that everyone makes, we all
are sinners,

Born that way in life is our only
beginning.

From then on we are to choose which
way is right and wrong,

With this body we have, flesh can
have its best, but our spirit strong.

Taking a beating of what life has to
give and survive the outcome,

Means there is a purpose for you, if
you accept what has been done.

Noted, is to what our body can
produce and keep on living,

But the "why" behind that reason is that God is not deceiving.

He has a purpose for you in life no matter what shall arise,

Just know that He is honorable and loving, that we should not despise.

Having the Holy Spirit in us can lead us in the right direction,

As long as we listen and follow, there will be no complication.

Sure we'll have our ups and downs, lefts and rights,

But we know we will always put up a respectful fight.

Always listen to God as he always hears you,

Then you'll never fail, but surely know it's true.

If it's meant to be in your life, then so be that as it may,

Remember that the Lord is in control, so shall you always obey.

Forgiveness

When you have the trust in someone
that isn't to be broken,

It hurts when it breaks and words
aren't easily spoken.

That pain blazes up like a fire from a
spark,

Not knowing if you can replace that
trust broken apart.

Knowing in your heart you have this
friend at your side,

You think you know who they are
until temptation sets it aside.

They make mistakes that at times is
hard to release,

It feels like a pain you have that
grows like a disease.

Once you shatter that area in your life, you have this barrier up,

That you don't know if you can let down again, beings they were so corrupt.

Some people can just let it go and let it ruin their relationship,

Others stick with their friend and build that trust up again, with no guilt trip.

It takes so long to build that trust but so easy to destroy,

Being loyal isn't an easy thing to do but when you are, enjoy.

The foundation of it can be unbreakable if you apply,

Only if you don't accept defeat and try to deny, hide or lie.

If you find it in your heart to forgive those who betray,

You will be the bigger person and not turn your back away.

But don't be played like a fool if you know they will strike again,

Open your eyes to see who they really can be, but you be the true friend.

Friends

What do the closest friends mean to
you?

When they've been there with
everything you've gone through.

It's not just another somebody that
you've done things with,

It's someone you love like a brother or
sister, that's the gift.

When you're down and don't know
where to turn,

A true friend knows how it feels and
has a concern.

Who will always be there in your time
of need,

To know that someone is there when
you bleed.

You have all the laughs in the world with that person,

To have him or her be there in times of desertion.

Shows that a true friend will never give up you,

Their hearts will forever be open to a mirrored friend, you.

If anything was to ever happen to your friends,

Even if the smallest thing corrupted the end.

And you didn't have a chance to say good-bye,

That would forever be lived with 'til the day you die.

Not to ever have friends in your life would be a regret,

You wouldn't have anyone to have an outlet.

With moments together that you'll never forget,

Would be something you'd miss out on if you did.

Godsons

Going through life never knowing
who'd be there,

Having that someone there who
listens and cares.

Until you find someone you trust with
your life,

Is someone God gave you to have,
never to say good-bye.

Holding on to someone for so long and
to be so close,

To consider each other brothers is
earned not chosen.

Having the title of godfather of his
children,

Means more to me than my own life,
that, I would give.

Having them here has made me a
better person,

Fighting for things I never would
have done.

Realizing things around me has
changed,

Knowing in my heart, things will
never be the same.

As I watch them grow in my own
eyes,

Not knowing what life brings as a
surprise.

Teaching them right from wrong is a
must,

Having them learn from mistakes and
such.

Good and bad will always be lingering
around,

Choosing the right thing to do is solid like the ground.

Growing from the wrongs made through life,

Will make them stronger and wiser without a try.

Having them see me as someone who will never let them down,

Will forever have a comfort in my heart and soul without a doubt.

Having their trust in me will always be treasured,

Nothing in life can break that, nothing can be measured.

Making my own promises to them I will always keep,

Never letting them down with words I speak.

I will always look after them with love and care,

Treating them as my own, I will forever be there.

Heavens Angel

When two people bring a child into this world,

No matter whether it's a boy or a girl.

Happiness is filled with unspeakable emotion,

Always to show you care with endless devotion.

The blessing that is brought upon this earth,

Is more valuable than what gold is worth.

As overwhelming as it may come to be,

Struggles will arise for you to overcome to see.

Seeing that child, you can't express with words alone,

The feeling inside that we will always show.

No matter what we do or how hard we try,

The amount of love we have will show from the inside.

Making them promises that we are to uphold,

Following through with them and not let it go.

Proves to yourself and to that child,

That they can trust you with a smile.

Watching them grow through the years to become a man or woman,

Thinking back, feeling as if it all has just began.

Seeing them accomplish their goals in
life,

Makes you feel happy and proud to be
alive.

As we get older and our days come to
an end,

Leaving behind you child or children
to start a new life, begin.

We see a place with streets paved
with gold and freedom

There we know we are somewhere in
a place with Jesus.

Hiding Eyes

Every time I look in your eyes,

It seems like you have something to hide.

Never knowing what's on the inside,

It sometimes look like you want to cry.

Trying to bring the truth inside out,

Is harder than it seems, you just want to shout.

I only seem to be able to see the outer you,

But what's on the inside is something new.

Figuring out what lies beneath,

Never wanting your feelings to retreat.

Bringing you out to the surface,

Always wanting your feelings to have a purpose.

Even though you'll never show certain pieces of your heart,

I will never try to break them apart.

All I want and all I ask is to see the real you,

With nothing to hide behind your eyes, always revealing the truth.

Your eyes are the window to your soul,

May your true feelings for me forever show.

If I can see past the whole exterior,

With no secrets to hide on the interior.

Hope & Faith

What do you do when you're down
and out?

When you feel life has betrayed you
without a doubt.

You want to go down a different road,
take another route,

One where you don't feel like you
want to cry, scream, shout.

Everything in front of you seems to
slip away,

Inside it feels like it's all turning gray.

Holding on to the last bit of hope you
feel you have,

Looking in every direction for what
you can grab.

Finding yourself lost with nobody else
around,

As the world at your feet slowly
crashes down.

Trying to keep all your emotions from
being confound,

With everything piling up, it just
seems profound.

Having faith is hard to uphold,

Even when life can be so bold.

Keeping hope in what you believe,

Sometimes can set your mind at ease.

No matter who you are or how you
live,

You should thank God for the blessings
you get.

Life is going to throw many obstacles your way,

Just keep your hope and faith up while you pray.

Left Behind

Young, living life to the fullest that
you know how,

Doing things that seem cool, fun and
real in the now.

Not thinking about what is and what
could never be,

Just going with everything in its own
ecstasy.

Feeling in a place where you're
completely safe,

Nothing can come between you in
that certain place.

A rush of feelings overpower you to a
point of no return,

You let them take over like a fire
spreading as it burns.

Decisions come into play even when it's too soon,

Then you find out the result and you shake and swoon.

Having to tell your significant other can be hard to swallow,

Even though you'll know that he'll be there to support, follow.

When you tell him what's to come, in his eyes you stare,

The painful remorse and fear that you both share.

You never would think to feel the same as he does, with such despise.

It's more to handle than you ever came to realize.

The overwhelming sigh that comes from the wave of shock,

Seems like everything gets silent, as if
the hands of time have stopped.

Struggling with thoughts as it breaks
you down mentally,

The consequences to be endured
doesn't seem worth it to me.

When it's all too much to take in and
you have to decide,

You give in to the fact that you're
unable to set aside your pride.

To go through the process, as
heartbreaking as it is,

Nothing in life could be harder to
handle more than this.

Leaving behind a soul that was soon
to be a miracle,

Hurts deep to watch something so
precious and beautiful,

Be wasted away from a selfishness act
and with no regard,

That alone will forever leave your
soul with painful scars.

Life As It May Be

Being young, putting perspective on this life,

Living on day to day and from night to night.

Only to see one way to live, though one knows it isn't right.

Wondering if I'm able to stand on through this fight.

Thinking there will be nothing to ever worry about,

When the time comes to grow up and live throughout.

This life we have is forever with us, with no doubt,

Knowing there will always be someone we won't live without.

Waking up to a brand new day with
innocent eyes to the world,

Seeing the day surpass, living through
the twists and twirls.

We grow never knowing what's going
to happen around,

Until one day we realize we can walk
on solid ground.

We feel as if something is wrong and
out of place,

Moving on with moments to look back
on, but never to retrace.

Holding on to another day, reaching
out for a last ray of hope,

Catching a glimpse of years gone by,
learning to live with life and cope.

Struggling to live another night on
this earth,

Facing this life we have and what it's worth.

While the day seems to slowly pass,

With no remorse with what I have to relapse.

Looking on to see another light of day,

Pondering if it'll be in shades of gray.

As we look to the sky above our heads,

Thinking it would be better off there instead.

<u>Lost</u>

When you don't know which way to turn,

When you don't know who will be there with concerns.

Things seem to all fall apart,

It all feels like it ends with no start.

Standing alone in an empty place,

You think that life is nothing but a disgrace.

Looking at things through black and white,

Wanting to see it all through a clear sight.

Searching around for an answer within,

Through this life that I am given.

But it all seems like that I'm dreaming,

All I know is it's my life I'm living.

Trying to open my eyes to my inner self,

Knowing that I've been blinded by myself.

Seeing things about me I never realized,

Never thought that I'd see that side.

Am I only to blame for this life?

Is it something that has been blind-sided?

Has it been forced upon me?

Or am I what I am to make it out to be?

Being lost with not knowing what to do,

Finding an answer with everything true.

Looking up with an amount of faith,

Striving to carry on to see a better day.

Misery

This anger on the inside is something
hard to deal with,

So built and bottled up I feel like it's a
myth.

It's eating me alive and I don't know
how to handle it,

Afraid to let it show, knowing I'd
regret.

The things I might say or things I
might do,

Would hurt me more than it would
hurt you.

Being lead in the wrong direction,

Not having the inside protection.

With the pain right along its side,

I don't know if I'll ever feel alive.

Sometimes I think that it'd be better to just curl up and die,

With unanswered questions with answers of "why?"

Not being alive and living with all this agony,

Would be better off than going on through life weary.

But knowing God is here by my side, always here with me,

And keeping me standing here on my feet.

Missing You

Sitting here not knowing what to do,

When all I can think about is missing you.

With these thoughts going through my head,

I know they're things I should forget.

Being this far apart is unbearable to stand,

Always wanting to be with you, every way I can.

When my heart beats for my one and only,

I hope your heart beats too, only for me.

My eyes light up when I hear your voice,

Even more when I see you face, more
beautiful than before.

Your eyes let me know how you truly
feel,

I still can't believe it, it just seems to
be unreal.

The tears we've cried with moments
we've shared,

Shows how true we are to each other,
with so much care.

Never to forget the words I have said,

They are spoken with honesty never
to regret.

Mother (pt.1)

M...is for the many times a mother is always there for you in times of need.

O...is for the obstacles they embellish when the hard times of life begins to bleed.

T...is for the ways she is terrific in all aspects of life.

H...is for her unconditional love she gives when there is strife.

E...is for ethnical teachings she brought into our minds.

R...is for how she remembers the best of you and leaves the rest behind.

Put them together, you have the one person who will never leave your side,

Forever to love and cherish you with no regrets, even when we make mistakes in life.

Mother (pt.2)

What does a mother mean to you in life?

To me, it's someone who always stands by your side.

Through thick and thin, she is always behind me.

Having my back when I'm in times of need.

She was there in the beginning and she'll be there in the end,

With all the trials and tribulations we face, even with the sin.

She'll forever be by our side, regardless of the circumstance,

I know she will never give up on me, giving me another chance.

Time after time, mistakes are being made,

It breaks her heart but I know there's more I could've gave.

Doing things that I know I should've resisted,

Having her there will always be persisted.

The tears that she has cried for me will not be forgotten,

It pains me to know that I caused her that, with all she's taught.

Wisdom and correction she gave me, I will forever treasure,

I see her not only as a mother, but a best friend to treasure forever.

A true mother will never give up on her children,

No matter what happens or what road they begin.

She will always be there with her support,

And never dismiss you and never shall she abort.

<u>My Angel</u>

When I'm lying in bed at night, you're
all I can see

Thinking about my one and only and
what you mean to me.

My love for you will be always true
and may it forever be,

Your love for me I never knew until
you fell in love with me.

Thoughts blossom with a smile so big,

A small laughter forms from within.

The times we've had and things we've
shared,

Only to have those moments always
with care.

With you in my life is the best thing
ever,

Always wanting to be with you, now
and forever.

You make me as happy as I would
have never known,

I want our love to always be there
with room to grow.

The joy I feel can never be matched to
nothing else,

You always know how to make me
smile and melt.

When everything just seems to fall
apart,

You're always there to see the ways of
my heart.

For you to feel the same as I do,

Means more to me than anything I
find true.

Knowing you love me for who I am
with no looking back,

I see that as something special, as a
selfless act.

Loving someone so much I thought I
could never do,

Having the love given back only can
be from you.

Being together is far better than being
apart,

When we know we have each other
with each other's heart.

Never Known/Faded Memories

Having grown up around my family,
thoughts of them I never knew,

The times I had with them I rarely
remember as I grew.

Time went on and I never saw them
again, removed,

Memories I have, they begin to fade,
for them I never knew.

Seeing pictures and hearing stories of
the kind of people they were,

Makes me regret not ever taking
advantage of the time I had to get
closer.

Now is a time I wish I could take
back, but I can't, so what am I to do?

Move on through life and know they
loved me as well as they did you too.

I've done things in my life that wouldn't have made them proud,

Now I'm grown and I can't take back the past, why did I have that stuff allowed?

If they were here today, I know they'd see how I've turned my life around,

And be happy about who I am now and what I've done on this earthly ground.

The lessons I've been taught from my mother is a way how she was raised,

The person I am today is because of her, they would have been amazed.

Seeing a man the way a man is supposed to be, not getting crushed,

Beneath the world itself and overcoming things that have been hushed.

Nanny, I love you and miss you even though I never had the chance,

To get to know either one of you in life, but I must advance.

Papa, I love and miss you too without knowing who you was,

But today, you both mean something in my life with a cause.

One Day

Seeing your eyes for the first time, O
my, how they shined,

Touching your skin with a gentle
touch from mine.

Looking deep in your eyes, I knew in
my heart, you were the one,

Forever did I want to embrace that
moment under the sun.

Kissing your lips with the soft passion
of mine,

Feeling your tender touch on my face,
how divine.

Holding you in my arms, never to
release,

Feeling your heart beat next to mine,
not to decease.

The pulse of our blood that runs through our veins,

As our hands intertwine, palm to palm, with no refrain.

Smiling as if nothing else matters in the world,

Knowing our love would always be safe and calm.

Leaving you in this world alone,

Knowing our love will always be known.

Will be forever in my heart full of care,

One day in heaven will we reunite, with our eyes a glare.

<u>One to Confide</u>

All of the times in life that you have
made mistakes,

When you feel like you are just at the
point of break.

Your mind bleeds with endless
thoughts of failures,

You don't think they can be released,
but can with prayer.

Life isn't easy and it's not something
you take with a grain of sand,

You stop to think no one is there to
listen and understand.

But you forget the one that is always
with us, no matter what comes our
way,

Life has its problems that makes us
feel like we want to be taken away.

The times when you feel you want to
be alone to let it out and cry,

You think there is no one around, so
your mind is weighed with heavy
denies.

When you want to have that
someone's shoulder there to lean on,

Never forget that there will always be
someone with you who will never be
gone.

Being overwhelmed with thoughts of
what to do,

At times they leave you breathless
with being confused.

They bring pain and sorrow of things
that have occurred,

Being it's whatever you have seen or
may have heard.

Things seem impossible to handle by
yourself,

Feelings become stronger as the day
passes itself.

So you try to reach out for a helping
hand, finding nothing but air,

There will always be one who will
forever be with you there.

Having doubts and never fully
understanding why things go the way
they do,

Being tested from day to day on how
we react to the obstacles that we run
into.

Is something we live and learn from
with growth that comes with it,

Showing ourselves that we can
overcome anything as long as we
faithfully commit...

To our Lord and our God who lives in us each and every day we live,

We owe Him everything we are with everything we have to give.

Overcome

When tragedy strikes and you've been
beaten down,

You feel like your whole world has
been turned around.

Not knowing where you're going,
dragging your feet on the ground.

Wanting to speak out but you can't,
not even to make a sound.

Being treated in a way you weren't
meant to be,

The trouble in your life for which that
you don't agree.

Waiting for the day that you can
escape the disbelief,

To go somewhere in life where you
find happiness with needs.

Looking at the situation from where
you stand,

Having that someone to be there to
hold your hand.

Not to have that person be there to
misunderstand.

But to be someone who's with you that
completes your plan.

Growing from the experience has only
made you stronger,

You will never repeat the same
mistake no longer.

Learning to stand back on your own
two feet,

Shows that you have come back to a
place meant to be.

Hoping that you will never fall back
in the same trap as before,

Letting yourself get that far down again, you'll be back in that war.

Listening to others help you get back your own foundation,

Focusing on that will get bigger and better for gratification.

Promises

Promises are words that are worth
more than gold,

Keeping your word to them is forever
to uphold.

Breaking a promise would break even
the strongest hearts,

It would forever separate you further
apart.

It takes a lot to build that foundation,
but so easy to collapse,

Almost like falling into your own set
traps.

Having a trust that is so honest and
true,

Is something that you can't replace or
re-new.

Breaking a promise is more painful than broken bones,

It hurts more than being the death of one being stoned.

Broken dedication out of one person's mouth,

Is like water in the heat of a drought.

Walking the border of your own promises,

Is like accompanying yourself with your own loneliness.

It never seems to satisfy others, never to be complete,

It's almost like wanting to accept defeat.

So always keep your word of promises you speak,

If you don't, it'll just make you more and more weaker.

Knowing you kept your word will make you feel good inside,

You'll remember the feeling of being humble and not belied.

Reflection

When we look at ourselves, who do we
see?

We really don't know until we search
within deep.

We all have an outer shell that we
reveal,

But inside of us all, there's a place
that we steal.

Being our self, no one may ever know,

But to reflect on what is real can be
hard to show.

The pain we hold so deep within our
soul,

It's just something so hard to let go.

Having people look at you with so
much truth,

Hiding so much we have, if they only knew.

Letting go of what sinks far below,

Is something we may never do, 'til we learn to grow.

Bleeding on the inside of our own self-reflection,

Is hard to run from even when we have direction.

Suffocating from the things we hold so discreet,

Sometimes we will often have to just accept defeat.

Regrets

Looking at myself in the mirror, I
don't like what I see,

Who I've become, what I've done, how
do I find relief?

I've become shattered like a fallen
piece of glass,

Putting myself back together will be a
troubling task.

Everything around me just seems to
fall apart,

Everything I do, everything I say, I
just want to fresh start.

Collapsing inside, I feel a hopeless
peace to resolve,

Crushing, pounding thoughts leave me
breathlessly involved.

Surrounded by people I love that have
no idea how I feel,

I feel like a thief in the night, waiting
to rob and steal.

For they see the same side of me
because I choose to hide,

I want to come out of hiding and come
clean on the inside.

Day by day, slowly but surely, I put
my broken self together,

Changing areas in my life that will be
stood by forever.

Doing this change is not only for me
but for those around me,

Having that sense of satisfaction will
bring me happiness to see.

Leaving this world as the person I
want people to know,

With all the things I've done, I might descend to the depths below.

But with Gods grace I know I'm forgiven and that will forever be known,

To Heaven I shall ascend to and be thankful with tears to show.

<u>Replace</u>

At times in life you do things that you
regret,

Things that you can sometimes
forgive but not forget.

It damages a part of us that we can
never get back,

Leaving a scar that is open for more
and more attacks.

Seeing the broken hopes and broken
dreams,

Thinking of why these things are how
they seem.

Feeling pinned up against the wall
with no room to move,

Waiting for someone or something to
come along and sooth.

Deep within our minds, we have the
imprinted memories,

Wanting them to fade away but they
just destroy our reality.

We make them the center of all
remembered mistakes,

Holding on to them tightly wrapped,
embraced.

Seeking this all around us, with no
answer to be found,

That's when we only have one way to
turn around.

Turning to God for the hope and needs
that we only dream,

Christ is always available to whoever
wants to run to Him, know what I
mean?!

Second Time Around

Going through life like nothing else
matters,

Not seeing that we are just growing
sadder.

Settling for things that just get us by,

Having another life besides this one I
defy.

Not having seen what I can have,
knowing it's there,

Is something I regret by not opening
my eyes, how do I bare?

Waiting for the day to come to pass
where I can change my ways,

Having the strength to overcome it
all, I find a challenge every day.

Struggling with everything that has been done,

Wondering how this life has even begun.

Standing in a place I want to change completely,

But knowing that I can't do it in secret, discreetly.

The change has to stand out and be known around me,

It has to be seen and stood by with stone set integrity.

Not falling back in what I use to do, but standing firm,

From all that has gone on, I will have surely learned.

Now that the day has come, I will have to fight to walk each step carefully,

Reassuring myself that I will not go back to that life, leaving it behind me.

With someone beside me or doing it alone, I mustn't cave in,

Knowing it's a time in life I don't want to see again.

Secrets behind the Truth

Somewhere within our past,

Are secrets that we never cast.

Deep inside we hold the meaning,

Of the truth behind walls and ceilings.

The pain that is held within our brain,

With the scars that are always to
remain.

Pain will eventually go away,

But scars will forever be the same.

Crouched down on my knees, looking
up as I'm knelt,

When I cry I feel my soul begin to
melt.

The hurt I feel so deep inside,

That tears alone will not satisfy.

To think of reasons why we hide,

Secrets we hold in our life.

To feel the pain, it hurts so bad,

Wanting to just cross that path.

Into a realm of the unknown,

Being here, I just feel alone.

Countless times you thought "what if?",

You expose the truth to people you are with.

It could be better than to keep the pain,

But the trust would be hard to regain.

To trust yourself is all you need,

So remember, the truth shall set you free.

Sights of Creation

Being here as a person, what wonders
am I to see,

Everything that has been created
under the sun to be.

So marvelous and breath taking are
things for our eyes,

Seeing them will have us realize the
creation with sight.

Walking along a riverbed, the smell of
trees, quiet of nature,

Hearing the water flow downstream
while knowing it's pure.

Seeing a deer prance through the
woods is life at its best,

To know there's more to experience,
not leaving behind the rest.

Strolling by a waterfall, oh how
beautiful it is to be seen,

With a rainbow in the mist, it's the
promise of God that agreed,

Not to demolish creation again by the
waters of the earth,

But to have the image of that means
there is a spiritual rebirth.

Having to walk by the ocean and
feeling the rush of the waves,

Being it is in the open, on a pier, or
watching them crash in the caves,

While hearing the splashes and seeing
the tides come ashore,

Oh how I want to stay there and take
it all in, yearning to see more.

Taking a hike on a trail that leads to a
place of peace,

Tranquility overtakes and leads
somewhere never to cease.

Coming to a clearing that overlooks
the formation with blowing winds,

Standing on a cliff that stretches over
the land, with a gleeful grin.

Sitting there with the sight of a
mountain in vision,

Wondering what beauty there is to
look down with life's decision.

How the sights of the world can
change ones outlook,

Living to see the experiences made
from Gods outlook.

Sometimes

Sometimes people can't see you for
who you are,

Sometimes they don't know how easy
you can scar.

Sometimes when people hurt you, they
don't understand why,

Sometimes it's far beyond what they
say that makes you cry.

For some it is just a way of letting go
of what harbors within,

For some it's a way they reflect from
someone else's sin.

For some when it's time to release
what they have built inside,

For some they do things they may or
may not regret in this lifetime.

Sometimes when you want to sit by
yourself with no one else around,

Is when you feel more comfortable
with life's shaky ground.

Then you gather your thoughts and
realize you're more than what they
say or do,

When you hold your head up high is
when you conquer their thoughts,
'being strong all the way through.

Sometimes when they knock you
down, you get right back up,

Sometimes when you look at them,
you see someone corrupt.

Sometimes then you can lend a
helping hand,

Sometimes it's better to take the high
road than to stay buried in the sand.

Souls

How do you know when you met your
soul-mate?

Is it when you find each other by fate?

Is it when you feel like you see
yourself in someone else?

Or could it be how you find what life
has dealt?

Could it be when both of your hearts
melt for each other?

Looking in past the eyes, seeing the
soul of one another.

Or a feeling of love that you can't
describe,

Taking a glance at the other side.

To love someone so much that you
would go to hell and back,

To forever hold them in your arms,
not ever to retract.

Walk to the ends of the earth and
back just for that kiss,

A feeling that will last for eternity,
which, will never perish.

Having someone in your life that
means so much,

Having that someone with that
special touch.

Or to have nothing to live for but that
someone,

To have it slip away will devastate
you as one.

Seeing a shed of a tear from your eyes,

To feel the emotion from deep inside.

Knowing how you feel and to realize,

What's going on in each others mind.

How it feels to have that someone
there to rely on,

To be there when everything seems to
go wrong.

Through the good times and through
the bad,

Standing strong together, side by side,
with nothing to lack.

Spirits of Emotion

When you're feeling an emotion,
things can play a factor,

Letting it take control of you, depends
on how you react.

Looking at different sides of the spirits
from within,

Let me share a few of them, where do
I begin?!

Feeling a spirit of happiness can bring
a lot of joy,

Such as wearing a smile on your face
with everything to enjoy.

Where no one can bring you down no
matter what they do,

Somewhere along the lines, something
seems to break through.

Feeling the spirit of anger may make a lot of mistakes,

When everyone around you sees it, they look at you with heartbreak.

You may not know it, but it can bring so much pain,

That when you think about it, things never seem the same.

The spirit of hate is never easy to let go,

Some people find it harder than they know.

Feeling that emotion, you might feel alone,

Never hold a grudge on someone or something we know.

Spirits of sadness, with heartache we can't deny,

With the tears that are shed from so deep inside.

Sometimes we think there's nothing else left but for us to die,

Fighting to live on throughout the days with our heads held high.

The spirit of fear is one we often feel,

Never to know what it may reveal.

Being scared with little to no faith,

Knowing there will always be another day.

Spirits of love can be very strong when someone's close to you,

Somebody who is always there, with arms wide open and always true.

Loving that certain person with so much of your heart, means more than the world,

Having that love given back to you in the same, feels as if you have everything to unfurl.

Having these spirits of emotion are a part of life,

You can't avoid them no matter how hard you try.

Just living through the trials and tribulations can be tough,

But getting through them you will grow without giving up.

Tears

Through each day I live, there's never a moment that doesn't pass,

I see your face when I wake up and feel a comfort that lasts.

When you are on my mind and in my heart,

A smile comes to my face to know that we're not far apart.

Night after night I close my eyes and feel so alone,

Tears start to fill my eyes, a heartache inside that has grown.

Thoughts of you fill my head and I know that we'll never be,

Able to hold each other, to have you by my side, filling emptiness within me.

Dreams of you seem so real, feeling
the softness of your touch,

Hearing your voice so lovely and
sweet, there's no one with nonesuch.

Listening to you I could do for a
lifetime, forever and eternity,

Knowing you're here with me makes
me feel whole with serenity.

The love we have is so strong, nothing
can make it break,

Pushing on from day to day for
someone so great.

Our faith for each other is so deep, it
will never diminish,

Holding on to the closeness we share,
it will never have a finish.

The Fight

Opening my eyes to another new day
of light,

Wondering what God has in store for
me this time.

Will I be challenged and tempted
through the day?

Will I have the strength to know to
walk away?

I've traveled down the wrong path too
many times,

Fighting this hill to have another
mountain to climb.

Temptations are all around us every
day we live,

Knowing what to do is what matters
without misgive.

The dark side overtook me for so many years I've lived,

Knowing in my heart I was doing wrong, needing to be forgiven.

The darkness is so easy to absorb upon this human flesh,

Discarding of it is tough to do, but needed to be refreshed.

Seeing the wrong of another through my own eyes,

Is a pain I get within my soul that eats me from inside.

Feeling the wrong is a total different experience,

That will become a scar forever remaining in my spirit.

Will this guilt I feel within ever come to rest?

Maybe after I give in to what the bible says.

Until then I'm just another lost soul looking to be found,

I know what I need to do to be honest, true and sound.

Giving my life to God above, whose Son died to forgive my sin,

I need that to have Him open my eyes to truly feel forgiven.

What I have been yearning for, for so much time,

I finally want to give in and give Him all my life.

So as I am here, down on bended knees and pray,

I want you to have my life and guide my every way.

Seeking you for I will no more,

I know you're here with me, I seek no more.

Thy Love

To bring forth thy love that my heart
foresees,

Is a love that I shall not deny from the
one that is she.

As an empowered force takes over
thee,

My love for her is far greater than
me.

Thy love is beyond prosperous and
true,

What my heart feels is nothing short
of loving you.

Seeking for a love that shalt always
show forth,

Seeing thou bright eyes, it will always
be worth.

Time should forever be and never to
decease,

Her tender and loving eyes filled with
memories.

Finding her upon one lonesome
ground I walk,

Looking at thyself with eyes in tears
as I talk.

Thine heart bleeds for which you
beauty lies within,

For not to undergo anymore pain that
sits in sin.

Willingly I never want to deplete this
life thy shall live,

Forever being together will greatly fill
thine heart again.

Touched by an Angel

The smile on your face, I want to
always see,

Me smiling back at you I want to
always be.

In a place so dark and a place so cold,

The sparkle from your eyes bring light
to my world.

Your beauty is so natural far beyond
belief,

It makes me tremble from under my
skin beneath.

You are so loving, caring, precious
and giving,

You're an angel on earth amongst the
living.

The heart you have will forever be true,

That alone means more to me than I ever knew.

I will always treasure the person you are,

Even when there's time of pain and sorrow.

Never again will I search for my love,

Time and time again I thank the Lord above.

For bringing to me every dream that could be,

Hoping one day I can give my love, half as good as she.

The way we touch each-others soul,

No words could describe it other than whole.

The power it has reaches beyond the sky,

Through this time onto the afterlife.

Trapped

Walking this earth lonely and
disturbed,

Everything in its entirety feels so
absurd.

When it all surrounds you with
questions unheard,

Thinking life is worthless with
everything that's occurred.

Your mind is bothered and distraught,

While focusing on only one thought.

That you alone can't be sought,

Seeing yourself in a situation
forethought.

Feeling no one around you takes you
serious,

Everyone seems to be oblivious.

After you speak, you feel so lifeless,

To what you can bring to the surface.

Looking somewhere for a little healing,

Knowing you still have something to believe in.

Deep down inside you just want to start to cry,

For what you know that you can supply.

From deep beneath your eyes, where people can't see,

You're clinging on to life, holding on to it barely.

Being you, your self holds you responsible solely,

*For what happens in your life, so
weary.*

Thinking this pain can't be relieved,

But it can if you only believe.

That God, who you can receive,

*Through faith alone, if you try to
achieve.*

Valued Thoughts

When you lose someone close to you,

A piece of your heart breaks in two.

Thoughts begin to fill your head,

Of times we've had and things we've
said.

Memories that lie beneath the skin,

Are moments never forgotten from
within.

Every day I find to see,

The world surrounds me at my feet.

Walking this earth from daylight to
night,

Waiting for the day I see that special
light.

Sure the pain in my heart will remain,

And the love from you will stay the same.

Moving on from day to day,

Until the time comes to go my way.

To the sky I look with wonderful thoughts,

I know the Lord is with us through the twists and knots.

As Heaven awaits for our return,

I thank the Lord for all He's done.

<u>Wanting You Near</u>

As I sit here thinking of you,

Thoughts of love I feel true.

A smile appears on my face,

The kind of love we both embrace.

Standing alone under heavenly skies,

Wanting nothing more than to look in
your eyes.

Seeing the beautiful clouds, feeling a
gentle breeze,

May the time we have together never
cease.

With every step I take, it feels as if it
could be the last,

Without you by my side, I don't think
I could sacrifice.

Every day spent alone is something hard to do,

Knowing one day we'll be together forever and true.

Looking in the night at the moon and stars,

I think of how lovely they look, amazing by far.

Holding you close I would forever feel,

The love for each other will always be real.

Weight of the World

The weight of the world can be hard
to flee,

When it's on your shoulders as heavy
as can be.

You feel as if you just want your
spirit to float away,

Nothing can spare you from the pain
that lays.

Not to know what to do or what may
become,

Not knowing how to deal with these
feelings that succumb.

Trying to bury it all so very deep in
your mind,

You just want it all to end, leave it all
behind.

Hurting so bad your mind races with endless thoughts to reveal,

Unanswerable questions form where only you can feel.

Searching for a meaning for what it is that bears so deep,

Buried in the silence of thoughts you only find to see.

You want to cry out, but it'd do no good,

Shaking within, you want it to end, but you never could.

It'll only cause more heartache for others, yes it would,

How do you live knowing you can't go on to seclude.

Living in a life that holds so much resentment,

Trying with everything you have to have commitment.

You think you're a failure in the eyes of everyone else,

Wondering why you live and for what, besides yourself.

It's never good enough even for you,

You want to just give up and be through.

Why oh why do I feel this way?

Always thinking, "Should I deserve to live another day?"

But when I stop and look up to the sky,

I take a long deep breath and sigh.

Realizing that I am a child of God,

With reasons that I'm here is forever sought.

<u>What If? (pt.1)</u>

What if I wasn't alive?

Would it matter to the world?

Being just a mere thought that
survived,

In someone's mind they find
comfortable.

How much different would this place
be?

If no one ever made a mistake.

Would it be the same way it is now?

Or somewhere better off to forsake.

What if things didn't happen for a
reason?

How would it reflect on us?

Passing through this life with no other vision,

Seeing things happen, feeling so worthless.

How am I to be placed in this life?

When all I can do is just kneel and cry.

Am I to be happy and content with who I am?

Or feel like I shouldn't have ever even began.

What if people could care less who U am?

To the point where I couldn't give a damn.

Would it change the perspective on myself?

Or would I be just another book on a shelf?

To be just a gleam in someone's eye,

A mistake or blessing, with a final breath of a sigh.

When they didn't think about it for what it could be,

I don't see why that had to be someone like me.....

What if? (pt.2)

Would it have been better not to ever
been born?

Feeling like a falling rose petal or a
thorn.

Into such a life of sorrow and misery,

I wonder how many people would
agree.

I think this life I live is hurtful and
faint,

I have no one except myself to blame.

Wondering if someone can see it too,

For the way I am living with such an
issue.

Breathing can be a real task at hand,

When it all comes to a sudden stand.

Seeing life through these eyes I find,

Should I even be alive?

Sometimes I think being born into this life,

Is a waste of a couple peoples time?

Knowing I'm loved, brings comfort to my heart,

But what if....things were different from the start?

<u>So It Ends</u>

So as this chapter in my life ends,

This next one shall begin.

Going through this journey was an
adventure,

It will never be forgotten, that's for
sure.

Shedding so much pain,

But there was nothing more to gain.

Shedding out so many tears,

What more could I feel in the years?

Every day learning as something new,

There were times I felt this wasn't
true.

Growing from each experience in this
life,

Teaches me something more each day
I strive.

Looking forward to what's to come,

Waiting to see if there's more than
some.

To go through it all in life can have
ups and downs,

It's how you handle things around you
that makes you smile or frown.

Made in the USA
Middletown, DE
01 April 2023